"As a cc
practical   ...tes. Coach
Smith gi\   .. ciear, easy to read book. If you
wonder how you can do sport 'heartily as unto the Lord,'
The Christian Athlete tells you very clearly."

Coach Mike Stanley, Former Head Coach,
Miami University (OH) Wrestling Program;
Head Coach, Columbus Crusaders Football Program,
Columbus, Ohio

"Athletic competition, the drive for excellence, and the
desire to win often leads to controversial decisions by
athletes and ultimately poor sportsmanship. *The Christian
Athlete* gives a Christian perspective on competitive
athletics and a biblical approach to the challenges that
every athlete faces. Dwayne Smith presents a fresh
approach to the modern day challenges that have plagued
athletes and their support systems for years. He cites
relevant examples of problems in a number of sports with
solutions that are sure to strengthen both the athlete's
abilities and their Christian walk. His brief but relevant
'Evaluate Your Game' and 'Time Out' sections at the end
of each chapter provoke a time of reflection and devotion.
It is a must read for athletes, young and old."

Taylor Smith, Jr., Vice President of Executive Support;
Association of Christian Schools International,
Colorado Springs, Colorado

"*The Christian Athlete* is a highly entertaining book that holds your attention while empowering you with God-inspired principles for life at its best, on and off the field. Coach Smith speaks with power because he has lived the truth in it. As you read his book you will be inspired to think through your sports-game and your life-game as you seek God in real, practical ways on and off the field."

Jeff Dybdahl, Head Pastor,
Northside Fellowship Church, Westerville OH;
Founder/Director, WASA Eagles FC, youth soccer club

THE CHRISTIAN ATHLETE

THE CHRISTIAN ATHLETE

Honoring God
in Sports

Dwayne K. Smith

TATE PUBLISHING & *Enterprises*

Published by Tate Publishing & Enterprises, LLC
127 E. Trade Center Terrace | Mustang, Oklahoma 73064 USA
1.888.361.9473 | www.tatepublishing.com

Tate Publishing is committed to excellence in the publishing industry. The company reflects the philosophy established by the founders, based on Psalm 68:11,
"The Lord gave the word and great was the company of those who published it."

Book design copyright © 2008 by Tate Publishing, LLC. All rights reserved.
Cover design by Jonathan Lindsey
Interior design by Stephanie Woloszyn

Published in the United States of America

ISBN: 978-1-60604-812-2
1. Sports & Recreation: General
2. Religion: Christian Life: Spiritual Growth
08.12.08

ACKNOWLEDGEMENTS

All glory be given to God for His incomprehensible mercy, unfailing love, and amazing grace. He has blessed me with many talents and has multiplied those blessings by giving me an opportunity to share those talents with others.

Thank you, Jill, my lifelong love, for your care and support.

Thank you, boys: Luke, Kyle, Scott, and Chad for living out a childlike faith.

Thank you, Mom and Dad, for all of your wisdom and preliminary editing help.

Thank you, Jason, for your friendship and keen insight.

TABLE OF CONTENTS

FOREWORD

All one has to do is mention a great sporting event like World Cup, Super Bowl, Olympic Games, World Series, or a Final Four, and emotions start to run high. All over the world people are ravenous about their team, their sport, or their sports' hero. Sports have become a major focal point for the human race. This fact has provided a wide open door for Christian athletes, Christian coaches, and Christian fans to proclaim their personal faith in our great God and Savior, Jesus Christ.

We are blessed to live in a time in the world of sports when there are many very successful coaches and athletes who are taking a bold stand for Jesus in their given sport. We have teams praying at mid-field before and after games. We have coaches and athletes who are giving God the glory for their accomplishments in post game interviews. Through televised sports programs, radio, books, and videos, the Christian community has awakened to the opportunity in front of them to share the good news about Jesus. We are positioned to tell others not only how He has impacted our performance but how He has enhanced every aspect of our lives. The courage of these coaches and athletes to share so boldly has encouraged many other Christians in the sports community to look at their own opportunity and ask some important questions. "How do they do it?" "How can I live out my own faith in Jesus on my team?" "Where can I go to find the answers to my own questions?" "How can I help others to come to faith in Jesus and help them grow spiritually?" The short answer is God's Word, the Bible. This "Miraculous Manuscript" is God's blueprint for a life well lived. It will give all who venture into this unending source of wisdom and understanding a firm grasp on the life God blesses. Living out its precepts and principles will aid you in your desire to please God and be a blessing to those around you.

God has raised up in the sports community many men and women to teach coaches and athletes to participate in sports using biblical principles. There are a host of coaches and athletes who are willing to share from their own experiences dealing with success and failure. They often speak at clinics, conferences, and in local communities about their own spiritual journey with Christ. They have written books and tracts and provided videos to aid others in their quest to honor God in their chosen sport. For those who want to know, the information and inspiration have been provided.

Coach Dwayne Smith has provided us with a beautiful rendition of his own passion to coach with biblical principles. He has helped us make the transition from Bible knowledge to practical faith. Each chapter is short enough for an athlete's or coach's busy schedule but full of Scripture and real life examples that bring the Truth alive. *The Christian Athlete* is a much needed tutorial helping us to learn the principles then taking them to the field and "playing" them out. Coach Smith has done an excellent job of assisting coaches and athletes everywhere to participate in a way that honors God and brings glory to Jesus Christ.

Coach Daryl Bell
Coaches Ministry Director
Fellowship of Christian Athletes

INTRODUCTION

Grant Thomas' basketball team is getting its tail whipped by a cross-town rival. Grant is the team captain and the floor general. His teammates have always fed off of his energy and fire, but his performance on this day has been less than average, and he is starting to boil inside. He can't make a shot to save his life, and the man he is guarding, Chris Donovan, has nineteen points and is looking to score two more. Chris makes a brilliant crossover move, putting Grant on his heels. He drives, pulls up, and pops an eight-footer. The shot looks like it kisses the glass perfectly, but the ball glances off the front end of the rim, and Grant grabs the rebound. He is immediately pressured, so he swings his elbows to create some space and catches Chris just below the eye. The whistle blows. The referee faces the bookkeepers and announces, "Personal foul on…white, two, two."

Grant shouts, "Who? Me? You're calling it on me?"

"Watch yourself, son."

Grant positions himself to be nose to forehead with the official.

"You have to be kidding me! That jerk is all over me, and you are calling the foul on me?"

"Not one more word!"

"You are the most pitiful ref that I have ever seen in my life!"

The official chirps his whistle and slams his right hand on top of the fingers of his left hand forming a *T* and begins to walk towards the scorer's table to record the technical foul.

If you have ever played, coached, or even watched a sport, then you have probably witnessed this dramatic scene a few times, where the lack of self-control by a player or a coach results in a penalty, dismissal, or physical altercation. Maybe you have personally been involved in a similar drama.

In this day and age, competition tends to bring out the worst in people, and it is most visible in the world of sports. Athletes and fans seem to lose their social skill inhibitors and are compelled to do things that cheat sports of its purpose—of God's purpose.

■　■　■

Every sport falls victim to an individual's lack of self-control at times. There are always stories that hit the newsstands of famous athletes demonstrating their lack of respect for what sports are all about, from basketball to figure skating, from tennis to cheerleading.

What seems to be the motivation of these actions? How can I prevent this type of behavior from my teammates, players, and children? What is the true function of sports, and what is my role in it? Is it possible to hold fast to Christian values and be a competitive athlete? Is it acceptable to let Christian values slide during competition? Can the meek expect to be winners? These are the questions that led me to write this book.

They are some of the questions that I have wrestled with in my experience and development as a Christian in the world of athletics, as an athlete, coach, referee, and father with children playing the games I love.

It is my prayer that as you read this book, you will see your involvement in sports as God sees your involvement in sports. I pray that you make the most of your opportunity as a player, coach, parent, or fan to bring glory to Him and to direct others to join you in that endeavor. I pray that you will be encouraged to strengthen your God-given talents, develop godly character, and praise the Creator by presenting your talents as an offering to Him for His glory.

PART 1

A Talented You

Your talents are God's gifts to you. What you do with your talent is your gift to God.

Adapted Danish Proverb
—Dr. David Jeremiah

As simple as it sounds, we all must try to be the best person we can: by making the best choices, by making the most of the talents we've been given.

—Mary Lou Retton

GOT TALENT?

Growing up, my friends and I used to play anything and everything in the street. We had bike races and skateboard races, played street football, kickball, and tag. You name it, we did it, and we had a blast… except when Max and Mudgie were running loose. Max was a 200-pound German shepherd, and Mudgie was a 200-pound black lab. I am sure they weren't really that big, but that is what it seemed like at the time. The dogs were supposed to be penned in their backyard by an eight-foot fence at all times, but they had no problems jumping over it or digging under it whenever they wanted to feed on little kids. That was the legend anyway. Their favorite pastime was to dig up large stones, chew on them until their gums bled, and then carry them around in their mouths with their lips raised so we could see blood dripping between their sharp teeth. The sight of them scared us half to death. So when someone screamed, "Max and Mudgie!" there would be twenty neighborhood kids flying out of the street.

One summer afternoon we were playing kickball in the street, and my younger brother was out with us. He was four or five at the time, which means I was ten or eleven, the age of most of the kids out that day. We were having a great time until we heard the dreaded scream, "Max and Mudgie!" The two ferocious beasts were coming from their yard up the street, giving us only one direction to run. We took off. I was running as fast as I could, so it was a bit of a shock when I looked up and saw my little brother (with the fear of death in his eyes) pass me and proceed to lead the pack. He was flying down the street, "bookin' it," as we used to call it. My little brother was fast. I'm talking Forrest Gump fast.

The dogs did not get to feed on anyone that afternoon, but my brother revealed to all of us neighborhood kids one of his hidden talents. He grew up to run track and cross-country in high school, and he ran track in college. I think he could have made it to the Olympics, but the Olympic committee wouldn't allow Max and Mudgie on the track.

You might not be a fast runner like my brother, but you are an extremely talented person. There is no doubt about it. Some of your talents are obvious to you…some are not. In this chapter I want you to focus on the abilities you have that are not generally viewed as talents.

■ ■ ■

We generally liken the term *talented* with such words as impressive, incredible, or amazing. For example, if we hear that someone is a talented gymnast, then we might picture a person flying around the gym while others watch in awe of what he or she can do. We would expect to be impressed with their God-given abilities. A *talented* golfer amazes the average hacker with his or her ability to consistently place the ball in the fairway or on the green.

Remarkable abilities are not limited to the sports

world, but are in all areas of life. A good CPA is a *talented* accountant. A gifted orator is a *talented* speaker. The term *talent* is an expression we commonly ascribe to someone whose skills are amazing.

I want to challenge you to look at all of your abilities more closely and see how talented you really are. God has given all of us incredible abilities to do amazing things. The simple fact that you are reading these words indicates that God has blessed you with some tremendous gifts and abilities. Unfortunately, we take for granted our amazing talents and abilities, and we perceive them as ordinary instead of extraordinary.

Let's modify our general understanding of talent and define it as an amazing ability granted to someone by God to do something for the sole purpose of bringing glory to God. With this as our definition, then breathing must be seen as a talent. Walking and talking are talents. Even now the network of millions of neurons in your brain is celebrating its talent by firing impulses and transferring chemical neurotransmitters to interpret, analyze, and store the words on this page. When you consider the details of your earthly shell, you have to admit, you are a talented person. The bodies that God has blessed us with are truly amazing. King David said it well.

> You made all the delicate, inner parts of my body and knit me together in my mother's womb. Thank you for making me so wonderfully complex! Your workmanship is marvelous—how well I know it.
>
> Psalm 139:13–14 (NLT)

Our lives depend on us using the intricate blessings from God to do every activity under the sun. We talk, eat, sleep, and think because we have been blessed with the ability to do so. And the fascinating thing is, by righteously using our marvelous talents, we honor our Creator.

I gave my father an insulated flannel shirt one year for Christmas. He put it on immediately after he opened it. I felt honored. And every time I saw him wear that shirt, I felt a sense of glorification because I gave it to him and he was getting good use out of it. Similarly, I believe that God is honored when we use the abilities that He has given to us. In fact, since we are His workmanship, I believe God is glorified by our very existence.

There is no doubt about it; you are amazingly talented. Let's take care to make the most of *all* of our abilities, no matter how commonplace they may seem, to bring glory and honor to God.

Evaluate Your Game

- Make a long list of all the talents that you have been blessed with, and take some time to praise your Creator for them.

Time-Out

Lord, I praise You for creating me with amazing abilities. You purposely made me with specific talents. Help me to never take them for granted and to use them to bring You glory.

GOLD MEDAL TALENTS

Talented athletes are not just those with extraordinary speed, strength, and agility. A talented athlete is simply an athlete who has been given extraordinary talents. And as we discussed in the last chapter, we all have been blessed with those. Now, what we do with those talents is up to us. Let's look at a portion of Jesus' parable of the talents:

> The man who had received the five talents brought the other five. "Master," he said, "you entrusted me with five talents. See, I have gained five more." His master replied, "Well done, good and faithful servant! You have been faithful with a few things; I will put you in charge of many things. Come and share your master's happiness!" The man with the two talents also came. "Master," he said, "you entrusted me with two talents; see, I have gained two more." His master replied, "Well done, good and faithful servant! You have been faithful with a few things; I will put you in charge of many things. Come and share your master's happiness!"
>
> Matthew 25:20–23 (NIV)

This morsel of scripture is incredibly rich. Take some time to read the entire passage (verses 14–28).

Although the use of the word *talent* in this passage refers to currency, Jesus' parable is not about using money to make money. It is about being ready to give an account upon Christ's return for the use of the provisions God has given to us. Let's substitute the word *talent* as it is used in this passage with the term *talent* as we defined it in the last chapter—an amazing ability granted to someone by God to do something for the sole purpose of bringing glory to God. Now, as we dissect Matthew 25:20 and 21, we gain insight on how God wants us to use the abilities that He has given to us. According to this passage, it is our job to acknowledge the ability God has given (*"You entrusted me with five talents"*), strengthen that ability (*"See, I have gained five more"*), and present the ability to the Lord for His good pleasure (*"Come and share your master's happiness"*). We find the same correspondence with the servant who was given two talents in verses 22 and 23.

The interesting thing revealed to me in these verses is the reciprocating joy between the master and both servants. What joy must have been felt by the master when he first gave the talents to the servants? I know the joy that I feel when I give gifts to others. I am sure the servants experienced joy as they saw their talents starting to multiply and anticipated the joy that the increase would give the master. Imagine the joy that the servants felt when they were able to exclaim, "See, I have gained more!" And the joy comes full circle when the master invites the servants to share in the delight that he receives from their gifts.

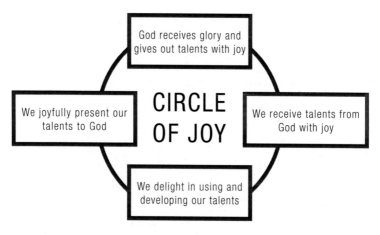

When we use the talents we have been given, athletic or other, to give God glory, we share the pleasure with Him. His glory and our joy are in harmony. They form a cyclical relationship that allows us to experience a joyful life. The wisest man who ever lived said it himself:

> Oh yes—God takes pleasure in your pleasure!
> Ecclesiastes 9:7b (The Message)

Have you ever listened to an interview of an Olympic Gold Medalist? The interviewer almost always asks a question about the athlete's workout routines. The response is usually something insane like eight hours of training, six days a week. All Olympians have incredible talent, but more than that, they have a deep desire to continually improve their talents. It takes an unbelievable amount of work to be able to stand on the top of a podium and be named the best in the world.

Our Creator gave each of us countless abilities. Some are common to all, and some are unique to one, but all are incredible. To take our abilities and make them gold medal talents requires training and hard work. The reward of hard work is pleasure; and remember–God takes pleasure in our pleasure!

> † Our Creator gave each of us countless abilities. Some are common to all and some are unique to one, but all are incredible.

Imagine that the five-talent and two-talent servants were athletes who trained extremely hard and made the most of the athletic ability that they were given. When the Master returned, we can picture them standing on a celestial podium receiving their gold medals as the Giver of the medals whispers in their ears, "Well done."

Evaluate Your Game

- In what specific areas of my *sport* do I need to train harder in order to attain God's gold medal?
- In what specific areas of my *life* do I need to train harder in order to attain God's gold medal?

Time-Out

Lord, I praise You for the joy of life. You have created me with such care. Help me to use my talents to their fullest, and may You find pleasure in my pleasure.

TALENT UNDERGROUND

There was another servant mentioned in the parable of the talents. He responded differently to the Master's gift. He was given only one talent to begin with, and instead of using it to gain more, he buried it. *Buried it?* Why? Let's look at it.

> Then the man who had received one talent came. "Master," he said, "I knew that you are a hard man, harvesting where you have not sown and gathering where you have not scattered seed. So I was afraid and hid your talent in the ground. See, here is what belongs to you."
>
> Matthew 25:24–25 (NIV)

The man said that he buried it because he was afraid. Afraid of what, I wonder? I might speculate that, like many people, he was afraid to fail. He may have had some experience with managing money, and he knew that he was not very good at it, so he avoided it all together. According to Matthew 25:15, the Master knew that he was not the best at managing money. In fact, of the three servants, he was the worst. It says, "To one he gave five talents of money, to another two talents, and to another one talent, *each according to his ability*" (NIV).

Let's put ourselves in the shoes of these three servants. God has given each of us an immeasurable amount of talents that we can place into the same three categories found in this parable. Consider the things at which you excel as part of your "five-talent" abilities. The things at which you are average are considered your "two-talent" abilities, and the things at which you are poor are your "one-talent" abilities. If we focus on our "one-talent" abilities for a minute, then it may be a bit easier for us to relate to the idea of burying a talent. For example, I am a terrible reader. I can read, but I would have to place my reading abilities in the "one-talent" category. It takes me forever to read a paragraph with full comprehension. That is one of the reasons why the chapters of this book are so short. When I was in school, a book report was the equivalent of jabbing a pencil in my eye. Reading was such a struggle for me, so I avoided it whenever I could. I rented videos, I got Cliffs Notes ®, and I rarely read my Bible. I did anything I could to elude spending the required time and energy it took for me to read a book. I spent a lot of time *burying* this talent.

The ironic thing is that God gave me the ability to read so that I can share in his joy. By burying that talent, I was indirectly saying, "Your gift is worthless, and I refuse to enjoy it." Is that not a slap in the face? God gave us the talents we have for a specific purpose. So, not only do we insult God by not using them, but we also deprive ourselves of the joy God desires to share with us.

> ✝ *God gave us the talents we have for a specific purpose. So, not only do we insult God by not using them, but we also deprive ourselves of the joy God desires to share with us.*

I have coached athletes with one-talent abilities in fitness. It is a chore for them to get in shape. They hate to run, they hate to lift weights, and they get frustrated when they compare themselves to players with five-talent fitness. These athletes have a choice to bury their one-talent fitness or to increase their fitness ability and make the most of that talent.

You may have seen the movie, *Rudy*.[1] If not; it is definitely one that I recommend you watch. It is about a young athlete that dreamed of playing football at Notre Dame. He goes to a walk-on tryout, and because of his fighting heart and strong work ethic, against all odds, he makes the practice team. In the movie, Rudy was described as being "five foot nothin', a hundred and nothin', and without a speck of athletic ability."[1] In the same scene, he was praised for working hard and hanging tough with some of the best football players in the nation—as a practice player. That is making the most of one-talent abilities.

Not all athletes make the most of their one-talent abilities. I have had some athletes who refuse to put forth any extra effort to improve their skills. This type of talent burying frustrates me as a coach. It affects a player's status on the team, their playing time, and ultimately their enjoyment. Let's go back to the parable and observe God's response to the servant who buried His talent.

His master replied, "You wicked, lazy servant! So you knew that I harvested where I have not sown and gathered where I have not scattered seed?

Well then, you should have put my money on deposit with the bankers, so that when I returned I would have received it back with interest..."

Matthew 25:26–27(NIV)

...And throw that worthless servant outside, into the darkness, where there will be weeping and gnashing of teeth.

Matthew 25:30 (NIV)

In contrast to the reciprocating joy that we saw in the last chapter, we notice in these verses a broken and declining path that leads to separation and disappointment. The master did not ask for much. He just wanted a little effort, a little demonstration of thankfulness for the blessing He gave to the servant. Instead He got nothing.

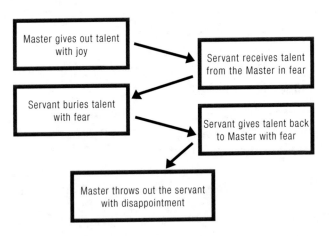

Broken Path of Separation

■ ■ ■

God has blessed us with the ability to strengthen and increase all of the talents that He has given us. Some of our talents are *five-talent* abilities that are easy to strengthen because we are very good at them. Some of our talents are *one-talent* abilities that will require from us a great deal of time and energy to strengthen. Regardless, we bring honor and delight to our Creator by joyfully using and developing all of our talents.

When you are on the court, in the water, on the playing field, in the classroom, or in the office, overcome the temptation of burying your weaker talents. Seek to develop them, and enjoy the blessing when you present the fruits of your labor to your Heavenly Master.

Evaluate Your Game

- What are some of my five-talent, two-talent, and one-talent abilities?

- In what ways do I bury some of my abilities?

- What can I do to increase the talents that I am currently burying?

Time-Out

Lord, I praise You for all of the talents that you have blessed me with. Grant me wisdom to find ways to increase my talents. Help me to avoid the temptation of burying your gifts to me.

PART TWO

Glorify God with Your Body

"You can see a lot by observing."

—Yogi Berra

GOOD EYE, GOOD EYE

Remember playing Little League baseball or softball? I can remember standing at the plate, staring at the pitcher with the bat over my shoulder. When the pitch came and a *ball* was called, I could hear my dad clapping and saying, "Good eye, good eye!" When I would watch a *strike* go by, he would clap and say, "That's okay! Wait for your pitch!" When I would swing and miss he would say, "Good cut!" My favorite cheer was always *good eye,* but at the time, I had no idea how profound that cheer was. God created us with the talent of vision, and all we have to do is simply raise our eyelids to use this amazing gift.

One morning when I was twelve years old, I woke up blind. I remember opening my eyes, and all I could see was a big white blur. I blinked, squeezed my eyes tight, opened them, and tried to focus—nothing, just a big white blur. I panicked, and I cried out for my mom. She rushed into my room and asked me what was wrong. I screamed, "I'm blind! I'm blind!" She told me to roll over on my back so she could take a look. When I rolled over on my back and looked up, everything came into focus. I was not blind after all. I had just woken up with my nose being an inch away from my white bedroom wall. I guess I was half asleep, because I still can't figure out why I did not look around before I called out for my mom, but I do remember being grateful for the ability to see.

■ ■ ■

I was shopping for a camera on the Internet when I came across the new Nikon D700. Whoa, you should see this baby: 12.1 Megapixel FX Format, broad ISO sensitivity to light, continuous shooting up to five frames per second, three-inch super-density VGA color monitor, rugged magnesium-alloy construction, dynamic integrated dust reduction system, and the list of bells and whistles went on and on. The purchase price was $3,000—a bit out of my financial league. The last camera I bought was a $70 special at Kohl's, so I couldn't even imagine buying anything like the Nikon D700. However, reading about that remarkable piece of equipment did get me thinking about two spectacular cameras that I do possess.

On my original birthday, my Creator gave me two state-of-the-art cameras. They are both sensitive to light, are always continuously shooting, and have large monitors that are only limited by my peripheral vision. They are magnificently constructed, contain a dust prevention and removal system, and the list of bells and whistles go on and on. Value: priceless.

I cannot begin to explain the complicated details about the eyes; from the lens, cornea, retina, cones and rods, to the optic nerve, to the seven different extraocular muscles in each eye dedicated to giving the eyes over twenty-five different movements. We simply raise our eyelids and take for granted that we can see.

The ability to use our eyes is one of the most amazing talents we have and one we should not take for granted. As athletes, coaches, or fans of sports, we must use this ability as God intended—for His purposes.

■　■　■

No matter what sport I participated in growing up, every coach I had would encourage me and my teammates to have vision. "See the field," "See the court," "See your teammates," "See the ball"…vision, vision, vision. God is coaching us in the same way; we must use our eyes for a heavenly purpose in and out of the playing arena. God wants us to have heavenly vision and see things as He sees them. To do this we must turn away from the walls that obstruct our view and look up to Him for guidance and strength. Any refusal to do that on our part will result in maintaining earthly vision, where all we see is a big white blur. We will remain blinded to the true purposes that He has for us in sports. Consider Paul's words in his letter to the Philippians.

✝ *God wants us to have heavenly vision and see things as He sees them.*

I'm not saying that I have this all together, that I have it made. But I am well on my way, reaching out for Christ, who has so wondrously reached out for me. Friends, don't get me wrong: By no means do I count myself an expert in all of this, but I've got my eye on the goal, where

God is beckoning us onward—to Jesus. I'm off and running, and I'm not turning back. So let's keep focused on that goal, those of us who want everything God has for us. If any of you have something else in mind, something less than total commitment, God will clear your blurred vision—you'll see it yet! Now that we're on the right track, let's stay on it.

Philippians 3:12–16 (The Message)

✝ *When our focus is on broken plays we end up missing the opportunity to touch broken lives.*

Often as a coach, I have had to stop using my eyes to critique the performance of my players and begin using them to actually see my players. How do they look emotionally? How do they look spiritually? That is heavenly vision. I encouraged my players to do the same with their teammates, opponents, and officials. It is heavenly vision that will cause us to give respect to others. We must see the people that are part of the game as people who matter to God, because if all we see are plays and calls, then we will miss what God sees. When we miss what God sees, then we can get easily frustrated and upset over the little things. When our focus is on broken plays, we end up missing the opportunity to touch broken lives. So let's keep our heads up and see what God is laying before us. Then we may hear our Heavenly Father clapping for us and saying, "Good eye, good eye!"

Evaluate Your Game

- What does God want me to see in my sport that I have not seen?

Time-Out

Before each game or practice, pray for God's vision.

Lord, thank You for the ability to see. Help me to see things as You see them. Use my eyes to direct me to do your will.

TAKE A DEEP BREATH

One of my favorite movies for pure entertainment is the 1985 film, *Remo Williams*.[2] In this film the main character, Remo, is being trained in the martial arts by a man named Chiun, the Master of Sinanju. For the first few days of Remo's training, Chiun focuses on teaching Remo how to breathe. Remo practices various breathing techniques in different situations; Chiun has Remo breathe as he sits in different positions, as he stands on high places, and even as he lies on his back while Chiun stands on his belly. Chiun tells Remo that if he did not breathe correctly, he would not move correctly. Now, before you run out and rent the DVD, please note that my friends often make fun of me because of the movies that I like to watch.

I have noticed that in many movies with martial arts as a theme, correct breathing is an essential part of the training. In fact proper breathing is the focus of every physical art or exercise designed to train the body. Watch any fitness video or go to any group fitness class, and you will always hear something like "Take a deep breath...inhale...and...exhale." You may be encouraged to raise your arms or close your eyes, but whatever activity is added, the goal is for you to relax by breathing.

Even now, whether you are focusing on it or not, you are breathing. Your diaphragm is contracting, creating an internal vacuum that draws air through your trachea, bronchi, bronchioles, and eventually to one of the 700 million tiny alveoli sacs in your lungs where diffusion separates the essential gases, putting oxygen into your blood stream and removing the carbon dioxide. Respiration is truly an amazing talent that we have and another one that we generally take for granted. Have you ever thought about glorifying God with every breath you take?

Chris Joseph, a high school girls' basketball coach, had teams who reached the Elite Eight of the Ohio High School Girl's State Basketball Tournament three times and the Final Four once. As an up and coming coach myself, I asked him how he helped his girls deal with the pressure of big games. His response was, "I tell my girls to breathe prayers." After chewing on that for a while, I grew more impressed with the wisdom that these ladies were receiving. As the girls played and their bodies required more oxygen, every internal organ naturally kicked it into gear in perfect synchronization to increase the oxygen supply so that they could produce and utilize more energy—not just to operate, but also to deal with the stresses of the game. Think about it. How often are we told to take a deep breath when we are stressed or under pressure? Breathing is the most fundamental form of relaxation.

Coach Joseph did not simply instruct his girls to breathe, but to breathe prayers. Prayer is the way we communicate with our Creator and Sustainer, and no one knows our bodies or our lives better than the One who made us. He tells us in His Word that the best way to handle life's pressures and stresses is through prayer.

> Don't worry about anything, but in everything, through prayer and petition with thanksgiving; let your requests be made known to God.
>
> Phil. 4:6 (HCSB)

With two words, Coach Joseph taught his team the two key ways to handle pressure: breathing and praying. How powerful must it be to combine the two—to breathe prayers.

I remember watching Coach Joseph's team play in a highly competitive regional game. The girls were giving everything they had out on the court, and I could not help but believe that when the pressure and exhaustion started to set in, these girls were heeding their coach's advice, and with each breath, they were letting their requests be known to God. They were calling on the Creator to give strength and endurance to the bodies that He created, so they could effectively use all of their talents to perform on the court.

In Rick Warren's book, *The Purpose Driven Life*, he described, "breath prayers."[3] He explained to his readers how to choose a prayerful phrase that could be said in one breath. Basically, every time you exhale, that short prayer comes out. In competitive sports, prayers may be: "You are my strength," or "This is for You." It could be a scripture reference like "Philippians 4:13," or a request like "Help me focus, Lord." Whatever the prayer, you are inviting your Creator to take part in your performance by giving your cares to Him.

> Give all your worries and cares to God, for he cares about you.
>
> 1 Peter 5:7(NLT)

> Always be joyful. Never stop praying. Be thankful in all circumstances, for this is God's will for you who belong to Christ Jesus.
>
> 1Thessalonians 5:16–18 (NLT)

✝ *Everything that we do, we can only do because of the talents bestowed upon us by our Creator.*

I am convinced that everything that we do can bring glory to God. No activity is too insignificant, not even breathing. *Everything* that we do, we can only do because of the talents bestowed upon us by our Creator. Inhale… and marvel at God's gift of respiration. Exhale…and never take it for granted.

Evaluate Your Game

- What phrase or verse could I use in competition as my one-breath prayer?

Time-Out

Lord, I praise You for the gift of breathing. Help me to glorify You with every breath I take.

TALK!

My wife coached a middle school girls' volleyball team for one year. She had never played it competitively on an organized team, but the school needed a coach, and she was willing. As I watched her girls play, I became repeatedly frustrated because the ball kept dropping in between two of her players. Their opponents hit the ball over the net, and as the ball approached them, they would turn and stare at one another, thinking that the other would make the play. "Talk!" was the collective scream from my wife and all of the competitive fans in the stands.

Effective communication is essential to athletic success. Communication with coaches, teammates, officials, and even opponents can directly affect performance.

God has given us a marvelous gift in the talent of speech. Our teeth, tongue, lips, larynx, vocal cords, and diaphragm all work together to allow us to form up to 140 different sounds. But our talent goes beyond just making sounds; we have been given the gift of forming words as well. Our words are one of our most powerful tools, and we have been given a great responsibility to use them wisely to bring honor to God. Hear the words of Jesus:

> But I tell you that men will have to give account on the Day of Judgment for every

careless word they have spoken. For by your words you will be acquitted, and by your words you will be condemned.

Matthew 12:36–37 (NIV)

Whoa. We are accountable for every word that comes out of our mouths, whether the word was reasonably thought out or just uttered without thought? That is a heavy responsibility, but it is a responsibility that we must accept because words are so powerful. That is why God has instructed us to use them with caution.

Careful words make for a careful life; careless talk may ruin everything.

Proverbs 13:3 (Message)

✝ *You never forget when you have been wounded or healed by someone's words*

I once heard a preacher on the radio say that words are living. He then went on to explain how words can affect the spirit like nothing else can and how they can stay with you forever. I agree. You never forget when you have been wounded or healed by someone's words, when you have been discouraged or inspired, humiliated or esteemed, deflated or energized. Words are powerful.

When I was in the eighth grade, I was one of the slowest boys in my school. I was a bit chunky, and on the surface I guess I did not look much like an athlete. My baseball coach at the time said something to me that I will never forget. He encouraged me to pursue avenues outside of athletics. He said, "You will never amount to anything in sports." Needless to say, those words crushed me. I will never forget them, and unfortunately, those words affected me so much, I never tried out for an organized baseball team again.

Two short years later, I was encouraged to join the high school track team—me, the slowest kid in eighth grade. The track coach was obviously not interested in my blistering speed, but he was interested in my growth as a person. He was committed to having his athletes learn life skills through the sport of track and field. He encouraged me and rained words of blessing on me. I fell in love with the sport and found myself transformed to one of the fastest kids in the school by my senior year. I even earned a track-and-field scholarship as well as a soccer scholarship to Huntington University in Huntington, Indiana. Words are powerful.

> Reckless words pierce like a sword, but the tongue of the wise brings healing.
>
> Proverbs 12:18 (NIV)

In 1988, my college soccer team was playing in the NCCAA National Semifinals in LeTourneau, Texas. We were facing the top seeded Eagles. At that time their star player was their left forward. His name was Freddy; he was quick, and he had a left-footed rocket of a shot and deceiving moves. I played the position of right back, so that meant that Freddy was my man—and I was up to the challenge. It was a hard fought game, and my team came up one goal short in the loss, but the most memorable part of the game for me was the battle I had with Freddy. Every time I tackled the ball away from him he would say, "Nice play" or "Good tackle." So every time he would get by me, I would say to him, "Nice move" or slap him five. Through all the politeness and kind words, there was a bruising, physical battle between the two of us. The words that were exchanged, however, demonstrated a mutual respect and inspired both of us to play at our best. That is the way games should be played. I loved that game.

God has blessed us with the amazing ability to talk. The words we use on the court or on the field can effectively enhance our play as well as be used to bless all of those in the game. We honor God when we use them carefully and wisely.

Evaluate Your Game

• How can I use my words to bless those involved in my sport?

Time-Out

Lord, thank you for the gift of speech. I pray that You will guide my words. Help me to use my tongue for Your glory.

NICE TOUCH

"Wow, she has a nice touch. What a drop shot!"

"He put that ball right into the receiver's hands. Boy, he has a great touch on the ball."

"Again, nothing but net—he has the shooter's touch tonight!"

These are just a few of the comments that we hear TV sports commentators interject when remarking on an athlete with a talent for finesse. These athletes have a five-talent ability to use the laws of physics to lob, sink, spin, drop, and bend a ball or a puck. They can brilliantly influence an object's disposition with the art of touch. But we are not on this earth to make an impact on mere objects; we are called to make an impact on people. Remember the calling of some of the early sportsmen, Simon and Andrew?

> As Jesus walked beside the Sea of Galilee, he saw Simon and his brother Andrew casting a net into the lake, for they were fishermen. "Come, follow me," Jesus said, "and I will make you fishers of men."
>
> Mark 1:16–17 (NIV)

I have been to several professional games for a variety of sports. I have noticed that they all have one thing in common: fans. Whether it is the NHL, NFL, MLB, WNBA, LPGA, MLS, or UFC, they all have people clamoring to see the elite compete. These devoted fans try to get as close to their favorite athletes as possible, reaching out their hands, hoping to be noticed and touched. With a little contact, a professional athlete can make an incredible impact that can send a young boy into a frenzy or make a young girl cry.

Touch is a fascinating talent. When we look inside the skin and muscle tissue, we find thousands of sensory receptors that pick up the slightest change in pressure or temperature. With a simple touch we can distinguish between rough and smooth, hard and soft, wet and dry, and hot and cold. We have countless motor neurons that we command and coordinate to activate specific muscles to push and pull, squeeze and release. With our nervous systems and muscular systems working together in perfect synchronization, we can swing, throw, stroke, and kick. We can shake a hand, give a hug, and pat a back because we have been blessed with the incredible talent of touch.

Touch is powerful. When used effectively, this talent can be used to uplift and restore, encourage and support. From simple high fives and fist bumps to more intimate hugs and kisses, it is the physical contact that expresses the value and affection you have for another person.

In concert with the right words, a touch is like an exclamation point that gives your words energy. Jesus often used touch with His words to uplift and restore.

✝ *...a touch is like an exclamation point that gives your words energy*

When the disciples heard this, they fell facedown to the ground, terrified. But Jesus came and touched them. "Get up," he said. "Don't be afraid."

Matthew 17:6–7 (NIV)

A man with leprosy came to him and begged him on his knees, "If you are willing, you can make me clean." Filled with compassion, Jesus reached out his hand and touched the man. "I am willing," he said. "Be clean!" Immediately the leprosy left him and he was cured.

Mark 1:40–42 (NIV)

God has given us the responsibility to be salt in this tasteless world. With His help we can use our gift of touch to make a positive lifelong impact on the people we associate with in our sports. Hugging a teammate, high-fiving an opponent, or patting a referee on the back could make a lasting imprint. But the best thing about using our talent of touch with others is, not only can we demonstrate the love of Christ to man, but Scripture says that we actually are demonstrating our love to Christ.

Then these righteous ones will reply, "Lord, when did we ever see you hungry and feed you? Or thirsty and give you something to drink? Or a stranger and show you hospitality? Or naked and give you clothing? When did we ever see you sick or in prison and visit you?" And the King will say, "I tell you the truth, when you did it to one of the least of these my brothers and sisters, you were doing it to me!"

Matthew 25:37–40 (NLT)

God feels the love we give when we touch the lives of others. The time we spend, the words we say, and the things we do can make a significant impact. Physical contact just adds a nice touch.

Evaluate Your Game

- Who in my sport needs to be encouraged by a kind word and a Godly touch?

Time-Out

Lord, I praise You for the gift of touch. Grant me the opportunity to use this gift to impact the lives of others for You.

PART THREE

The Battles Within

The battles that count aren't the ones for gold medals. The struggles within yourself...the invisible, inevitable battles in all of us...that's where it's at.

—Jesse Owens

There is nothing wrong with dedication and goals, but if you focus on yourself, all the lights fade away and you become a fleeting moment in life.

—Pete Maravich

BATTLING SELFISHNESS

> In the course of time, Cain brought some of the fruits of the soil as an offering to the Lord. But Abel brought fat portions from some of the firstborn of his flock. The Lord looked with favor on Abel and his offering, but on Cain and his offering he did not look with favor.
>
> Gen. 4:3–5a (NIV)

When I first read those words in Genesis 4, I remember wondering, *what did God want from Cain?* I mean, what was the big deal? Cain gave an offering, right? Should that not count for something? Why is the Lord so picky? Let me share a story with you.

My mom is a fantastic cook. She grew up in LaGrange, Kentucky, where she honed her southern cooking skills. Occasionally, I will remember a tasty dish that I had growing up and will call home to ask my mom how she made it. She always gives me the recipe and any secrets she has for the preparation. After specific directions she usually says, "Let me know how it turns out." Now, the best way for her to see how it turns out is for her to taste it. So whenever she came over for dinner and I was cooking one of her dishes, I got a little excited, and I would labor in the kitchen trying to make sure that everything was perfect.

My wife and I invited my folks over for dinner one evening, and I had the honor of preparing the main dish. It was boneless, seasoned, and breaded chicken breasts, smothered and simmered in homemade chicken-mushroom gravy. My mouth is watering right now. Anyway, on this particular night, I made a mistake, and the main dish turned out less than perfect. I burned the gravy (don't ask me how). Because the chicken was simmering in it for a while, it inherited the unpleasant burnt taste. Fortunately, I had enough time and ingredients to start over. The second batch turned out perfect, but I only had enough chicken for all but one person unless I used a piece from the first batch, which I did. My parents came over, and dinner was ready. I offered my mother the first piece and publicly acknowledged her part in the meal by thanking her for the recipe. Then I gave her the one piece of burnt chicken—a Cain's offering. Yes, I could have kept the burnt piece for myself, but I thought my mom deserved to have it since she did so much for me; she gave me the recipe and taught me to cook. You are right; it's absurd! Honestly, there is no way that I would do that to my mom, but that is what Cain's pitiful excuse of an offering was like to God.

What did God want? He wanted Cain's best! After all, God gave Cain the land to farm, the knowledge of farming techniques, and the ability to farm the land. He gave him over 700 muscles to move his 200-plus bones, which enabled Cain to move his legs, arms, fingers, and toes to plow and plant. God provided the nutrients and the moisture in the soil. He even created the crops that grew. Why would Cain have such a hard time giving the best he had to God? I suppose it is for the same reason we have a hard time giving our best today. We are selfish. Our sinful nature rears its ugly head, and we desire to be self-pleasing rather than God-pleasing. God does not change. He still wants our best and He deserves our best. And we should desire to give Him our best in everything we do because He gave us the talents and opportunities to do everything we do. We should give him our best by doing the best that we can. Like the poem attributed to St. Jerome says, "Good, better, best. Never let it rest. Until the good becomes better and the better becomes best."

All of the time that we put into practicing, playing, coaching, and even cheering must be seen as an offering that we are giving to the Lord. When we desire to withhold effort and we don't push ourselves to reach higher levels, then we are being self-pleasing and presenting a Cain's offering. We present an Abel's offering when we give one hundred percent in practices and games and leave the court or field mentally and physically exhausted, knowing that we have offered all we have. If we use our talking talent to selfishly ridicule, discourage, or put down others, then we present a Cain's offering. To selflessly motivate and encourage others is to present an Abel's offering that is a sweet and pleasing aroma to God.

> *We must battle the temptation to give self-seeking offerings, lest we become content with presenting God with less than our best.*

We must battle the temptation to give self-seeking offerings, lest we become content with presenting God with less than our best. Satan would like for us to fall into a false way of thinking–to assume that "okay" is acceptable to God. No, it's not. God wants our best.

I created a creed for the teams I have coached to memorize. I think it sums up the heart of an Abel's offering.

> *I am a warrior for Christ. My number one goal is to glorify Him, for He made me and He gave me my talents. So I will work hard, play hard, and fight to be the best. When I am at my best, people will notice, and in me they will notice Christ!*

God has given us so much. It is only right for us to draw on our talents to make every good thing we have become better…and to make our better become our best.

Evaluate Your Game

- Where in my sport am I presenting a Cain's offering to God?

Time-Out

Lord, thank You for the many blessings in my life. Help me to always give to You an Abel's offering. Forgive me for the Cain offerings that I have presented to You in the past.

BATTLING LAZINESS

Watching athletes for many years has allowed me to observe that deep down, most competitors desire to give their best, but not all are disciplined enough to do what it takes to be their best. The desire to be lazy is a tough battle to fight, and this internal foe poses a major problem for the *Christian* athlete because we that claim Christ as Savior should understand most that God deserves our best.

■ ■ ■

My father used to always give me the, "You're not just going to wake up one day and be great" speech. He might say, "Dwayne, you're not just going to wake up tomorrow and be an *A* student," or "You're not just going to wake up one day and be a great soccer player." I would just roll my eyes and continue to be mediocre in school and in sports. I was content in giving a Cain's offering in those areas of my life. When I look back at those teenage years, I get a little irked at myself. My dad was right. He was trying to get it through my thick teenage head that it takes hard work to be good, and it takes diligent work to be the best.

After years of coaching, I have come to realize that the core reason why athletes fall into lazy routines is due to the lack of understanding that in everything, they are presenting an offering to God. They fail to grasp the wonder of all of the incredible talents they have been given, and they do not appreciate those talents as being gifts from Him.

I get frustrated when I see an athlete refuse to put forth a worthy effort and become content to settle for mediocrity. I would get irritated as a coach when I could see a player's potential, but couldn't seem to break into that player's head and turn on the motivational switch to ignite a fire under them. I remember striving to find ways to make them see what they could be if they would just put in the work.

■　■　■

For wisdom in the area of laziness, Solomon encourages us in Proverbs to look at the ant, one of God's smallest creatures.

> You lazy fool, look at an ant. Watch it closely; let it teach you a thing or two. Nobody has to tell it what to do. All summer it stores up food; at harvest it stockpiles provisions. So how long are you going to laze around doing nothing? How long before you get out of bed? A nap here, a nap there, a day off here, a day off there, sit back, take it easy—do you know what comes next? Just this: You can look forward to a dirt-poor life, poverty your permanent houseguest!
> Proverbs 6:6–11 (The Message)

Have you ever closely observed a colony of ants? I actually heeded Solomon's advice and went out to find an ant mound. I knelt down and watched the tiny creatures intently. I picked up some brush, and I tried to block their paths with a stick, some grass, and a leaf. Nothing I did made them slow down, give up, or quit. If they were carrying something, they never put it down. These ants just kept working, and nothing was going to distract them. Then it hit me. They refused to be distracted! They were focused only on the task before them and that was it. These tiny creatures defined the term laziness for me by showing me its antonym (no pun intended).

> ✝ *Laziness is when we allow ourselves to be distracted from our goals or our assigned tasks.*

Laziness is when we allow ourselves to be distracted from our goals or our assigned tasks. We can be extremely busy or work very hard and still be lazy if our busyness or hard work does not target our objective—to be the best we can be. I have had athletes who will work diligently on their strengths but refuse to work on their weaknesses. That is laziness. Although they may be working hard to get better, by spending all of their energies on their five-talent abilities, they are actually allowing themselves to be distracted from developing an ability that will improve their game.

The key to overcoming laziness, as with any lifestyle problem, is to let our mind and spirit guide us and refuse to be distracted by the flesh. We must think like an ant, firm in our purpose, not allowing ourselves to lose sight of our goals. I like the way Eugene Peterson translates the words of the Apostle Paul in *The Message*.

> I don't know about you, but I'm running hard for the finish line. I'm giving it everything I've got. No sloppy living for me! I'm staying alert and in top condition. I'm not going to get caught napping, telling everyone else all about it and then missing out myself.
>
> 1 Corinthians 9:26–27 (Message)

I coached a high school soccer team that returned all of its starters from a state final-four appearance in the previous year. There were a lot of expectations placed on us to win the state title that year, and we were ranked number one in the state for the entire regular season. Ironically, it is easy to get lazy when you are on top. So, the common theme that I stressed to my players throughout that year was to remain focused on our goals and to refuse to be distracted. When circumstances arose that could cause a distraction (usually a strained relationship on the team), we dealt with it by reminding ourselves of our team goals—glorifying God, giving our best, and winning the state championship. The lazy tendency is to ignore the problems that distract us from our goals instead of dealing with them. We always regrouped and, like the ants, we stayed on task. That year it paid off—we captured the state crown and celebrated the title that eluded us the year before.

■ ■ ■

One of the biggest obstacles to hard work is the internal problem of laziness. It is tough to remain focused on our goals, but the benefits are worth it.

> Lazy people are soon poor; hard workers get rich.
> Proverbs 10:4(NLT)

> A hard worker has plenty of food, but a person who chases fantasies has no sense.
> Proverbs 12:11 (NLT)

> Wise words bring many benefits and hard work brings rewards.
> Proverbs 12:14 (NLT)

> Make it your goal to live a quiet life, minding your own business and working with your hands, just as we instructed you before. Then people who are not Christians will respect the way you live, and you will not need to depend on others.
> 1Thessalonians 4:11–12 (NLT)

Let's be determined to work hard with purpose in all of the areas of our lives. May we heed our Heavenly Father's advice and labor like an ant, because we will not just wake up one day and be great at anything.

Evaluate Your Game

- When do I become lazy in my sport? When do I become lazy in life?

- What are some practical things I can do to overcome my laziness?

Time-Out

Lord, thank You for the many opportunities you have given me to bless others with my gifts and talents. Forgive me for the times I have selfishly declined to work hard to be the best I can be for Your glory. Help me to work hard in everything I do.

BATTLING EGO

My two oldest children are twin boys named Luke and Kyle. From the time they were able to express themselves, they were demonstrating the nature of ego. Kyle said things like, "Daddy, I have my seat belt on, and Luke doesn't." Luke said things like, "Mommy, I brushed my teeth, but Kyle didn't." What they were really saying was, "Look at me; I am better than my brother." At a young age, my boys were jockeying for position in the family.

■　■　■

Even those closest to Jesus while He was on this earth fell victim to their egos as they jockeyed for position in their group.

> After they arrived at Capernaum and settled in a house, Jesus asked his disciples, "What were you discussing out on the road?" But they didn't answer, because they had been arguing about which of them was the greatest.
>
> Matthew 9:33–34 (NLT)

Scripture says that the disciples argued as to which one of them was the greatest. Each one was probably making a case for himself, listing the things he had done and citing all of the sacrifices he had made. I can hear the argument now: Andrew says, "Jesus picked me first, so I am obviously His favorite." Thomas answers, "Yeah right, I seriously doubt that." Matthew chimes in with, "Hey, I invited Jesus over for dinner." Simon replies, "Jesus came to my house too." James interjects, "Aw, that's just because your mamma was sick!" Huffed up, Simon fires back, "Don't be talking about my mamma!" Sorry, I'm getting carried away, but you get the point. There is an innate craving in all of us to be seen as better than others.

> † ...the problem of ego arises when our desire for recognition changes into a belief that we deserve recognition.

We all want to be recognized for something. The desire in itself is not wrong, but the problem of ego arises when our desire for recognition changes into a belief that we deserve recognition. The belief then turns into frustration if we do not get the attention we think we ought to have, and the internal frustration morphs into unacceptable actions when things don't go the way we want.

It is completely understandable why ego problems are so prevalent in athletics when you consider that the main goal is to work your way to the top of your sport. It is even more understandable when we add in the competitive and aggressive nature that characterizes most top athletes.

I believe that an athlete's fire, passion, and emotion are five-talent qualities granted to them by God to excel in whatever they do. Ironically, it is that very blessing of fire, emotion, and passion that can lead to ego problems on the field. These valuable characteristics tend to escape from the reins of the game and begin to target players, officials, or fans. They can become uncontrolled and subsequently evoke the egocentric mentality where situations related to games or practices are viewed through human eyes and not through God's eyes. This poor vision causes the Christian athlete to lose focus and forget that he or she is supposed to be modeling Christ.

Self-serving aggressiveness and competitive passion can be intensified if an athlete is a star and gets a lot of attention because of his or her talent and skill. It is difficult to remain humble when you are one of the best in a sport and are constantly being told how great you are. Instead of diverting the attention, you can actually start to believe in it, crave it, and demand it. That is when the ego problem manifests itself.

Another facet to the ego problem is in the person who perceives himself better than others perceive him. I saw this a lot as a coach. Players think that they should have more playing time because in their eyes, they are better than another player who is playing. Their ego then takes their focus away from the team and places it on themselves. They get frustrated, and the battle within starts to cause trouble.

How do you know you are battling ego? You know it when you are craving attention, and any glory that you do receive does not find its way back to God. It is when you are determined to plow your own rough, dead-end road off of the paved path of praise that leads to the One who truly deserves the glory.

The misdirected path of praise starts with God, the Giver of talent. The talent draws the attention of others. The attention feeds the ego, and then ego demands more attention and keeps the focus away from God, the Giver.

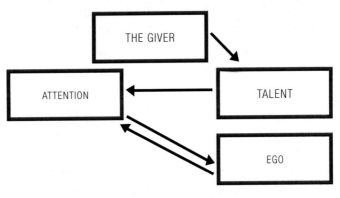

Misdirected Path of Praise

How should a Christian athlete handle the ego problem? It requires a humble heart and a servant's attitude. The key is to remove ego out of the way and channel the attention back to the Giver. The best part about humility is when you divert desired attention toward God; He lifts you up and directs it right back to you.

> Humble yourselves before the Lord, and he will lift you up.
>
> James 4:10 (NIV)

> He sat down, called the twelve disciples over to him, and said, "Whoever wants to be first must take last place and be the servant of everyone else."
>
> Matthew 9:35 (NLT)

Only when you have a true understanding of where your talent comes from and make it your purpose to glorify God, will you embrace humility and complete the path of praise where the Giver of your talent becomes the focus of the attention. The praise is redirected to Him, and there is no room for ego.

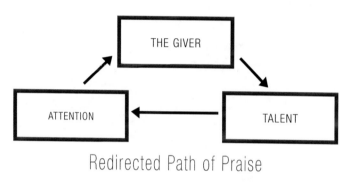

Redirected Path of Praise

Evaluate Your Game

- How can I remind myself that I am nothing without God?

Time-Out

Lord, help me to be humble before you. May others see You through me, for You are the reason for my successes, and You deserve the praise.

ACCEPTING PRAISE

This may seem a strange title for a chapter in this part of the book, but this has been a personal battle for me over the years. I have had a hard time with accepting praise. I have a good handle on my ego, but how far do I take humility? Is it okay to receive praise? How do I answer a compliment without sounding trite or rehearsed?

My struggle with accepting praise may have stemmed from my upbringing. I grew up in a pretty conservative church. At one point our congregation never clapped or showed the least bit of excitement for any performance from the pulpit. If a soloist or ensemble did an amazing job singing or playing a song, there was nothing but silent nods, smiles, or a quiet *amen* when they finished. It was awkward. Our hearts could be thrilled to witness the talent of these people, but we were subdued because we were taught that our praise should be given to God alone, not to man. I am not sure what changed, but my church is not like that anymore.

It is not wrong to want to be praised. After all, God desires to be praised, and we are made in His image, so it is only natural for us to also have that desire. We may not always deserve it, but the need to be praised is a true need.

■ ■ ■

I dabble in acting. Every year my church uses their collective talents and gifts to present the life of Jesus from birth to Resurrection in a spectacular Christmas concert and drama for about 30,000 people. We have live animals, incredible costuming, beautiful music, and a seeker-sensitive dramatic script. I have had the privilege of narrating the concert on several occasions, and I distinctly remember one year when my pastor, Jim Custer, came up to me and complimented me on my performance. I immediately deflected his compliment and said, "Praise the Lord." I will never forget Pastor Jim's response. He said, "And praise to the vessel He is using." I was worthy of praise because I was offering my time and efforts to God for His purposes. I was not wrong for saying, "Praise the Lord," because I truly meant it. But that incident helped me understand that when I perform my best with the talents God has given me and I receive praise for it, I can accept that praise. As long as I am giving the glory to God internally, I do not have to always publicly deflect the praise directed to me.

I do not believe that every athlete who accepts an award and says, "First I want to thank God..." is necessarily redirecting the praise to God. They may be doing it, but it is only significant if their actions on the field support that statement. We see it all the time—when an actor, musician, or athlete stands in front of millions of people and offers his or her thanks to God for an award that was just received for a movie that was not bringing honor to the Lord, or for an album with lyrics that did not bring honor to the Lord, or for play on the court that did not bring honor to the Lord. If the actions conflict with the words, then the underlining hypocrisy interferes with the praise supposedly directed to God. When it is genuine, however, it is true worship.

Take the 1999 NFL MVP for example. Kurt Warner was the starting quarterback for the St. Louis Rams and MVP of Super Bowl XXXIV. Throughout the season, Kurt consistently talked about the importance of his faith. After games, he was always seen in huddles of prayer. There was no doubt that he was a dedicated believer. When he was being interviewed after his team won the Super Bowl, he told a TV reporter, "Well, first things first, I've got to thank my Lord and Savior up above. Thank you, Jesus!" No one in earshot thought he was being hypocritical. Kurt Warner talks about this episode in his book, *All Things Possible*.[4] He reveals how *first things first* has become sort of a catch phrase for him because no matter what we do in life, it all starts with God.

Giving God the glory means two things. First, it means that you truly understand that without God, you can achieve nothing, and it is only because of Him that you are receiving praise. He gave you your talents and the opportunity to display your talents. Secondly, giving God glory means that you dedicate your best performance to Him. You give an Abel's offering in whatever you do.

Whatever you do, work at it with all your heart, as working for the Lord not for men, since you

know that you will receive an inheritance from
the Lord as a reward. It is the Lord Christ you
are serving.

Col. 3:23–24 (NIV)

We do not bring glory to God merely with words or
gestures. God is truly glorified when our hearts are
faithful to thank him for everything that He is and for all
He has given us. It is the internal praise that brings honor
to Him. If the inward path of praise is on target, then the
proper outward redirection of giving glory to God will
naturally occur because the by-product of internal praise
is external humility.

✝ *...the byproduct of internal praise is external
humility.*

Athletes who understand where their talent comes from
do not demand praise or attention. Athletes without this
understanding are the ones who spend hours coming up
with a celebration routine so when they score, they can say,
"Look at me! Love me, praise me!" Don't get me wrong;
I am not against celebrating, but you can celebrate and
still be humble if the celebration is simply an outpouring
of your excitement and not for your personal glory. An
outpouring of excitement is not preplanned.

I watched the Ohio State Buckeyes defeat the Miami
Hurricanes to win the 2003 Fiesta Bowl and capture
the NCAA BCS National Championship. There were
several things that I noticed about the Buckeye free-

safety, Michael Doss, that I found interesting. First, he made a key interception from Ken Dorsey off of a tipped pass and returned it to the Miami thirty-yard line. Was he excited? Of course he was, and you could tell. But, before he celebrated with his teammates, he made a quick and simple gesture to God by pointing to the heavens. Was it sincere praise? Only God and Michael can know that, but later in the game, the Miami star running back, Willis MaGahee, took a severe hit to the knee and tore three ligaments. Doss, with two of his teammates, were seen kneeling and praying for their injured opponent. Finally, the game ended with the underdog Buckeyes on top thirty-one to twenty-four in the second overtime. They interviewed Doss on the field, on the awards podium, and in the press conference. As expected, he was all smiles, laughing, screaming, and celebrating. He began each interview by saying that he gives "all the glory to God." I believe him, not because of his words. It was his attitude and actions during the game that convinced me.

The key to giving God the glory for all that we accomplish and for all the praise that comes our way, is to build a strong relationship with Him. It is in the alone time where our spirit is fed and our humility grows as we develop the understanding that we truly are nothing and can accomplish nothing apart from our Creator, Provider, and Giver of all good things.

Evaluate Your Game

- What are some healthy ways for me to demonstrate humility?
- How should I respond when I am being praised?

Time-Out

Lord, thank You for so many good things. Thank you for providing for my every need. Thank You for Your encouragement that comes from other's words of praise toward me.

BATTLING CIRCUMSTANCES

Athletics have a bizarre ability to unveil a person's sinful nature. It is the application of pressure in competition that causes people to let down their guard and allow their carnality to be seen. Consider Peter, one of Jesus' disciples. He felt the pressure when he was challenged about his relationship with Jesus in the midst of a tense and volatile situation.

> Now Peter was sitting outside in the courtyard, and one maid came up to him and said, "You were also with Jesus the Galilean!" But he denied it falsely before them all, saying, I do not know what you mean. And when he had gone out to the porch, another maid saw him, and she said to the bystanders, "This fellow was with Jesus the Nazarene!" And again he denied it and disowned Him with an oath, saying, I do not know the Man! After a little while, the bystanders came up and said to Peter, "You certainly are one of them too, for even your accent betrays you." Then Peter began to invoke a curse on himself and to swear, "I do not even know the Man!" And at that moment a rooster crowed.
>
> Matthew 26:69–74 (TAB)

Fear and anger was in Peter's heart, and when

unveiled, these hidden traits sired lying and swearing. Jesus predicted Peter's denial because He knew that although Peter was a good guy with good intentions, once the heat was turned up, he would not stand up and be salt and light to those around him.

You have undoubtedly witnessed this type of denial in your sport. It may not be as point-blank as or as obvious as in Peter's rejection, but we have all witnessed or experienced a scene where a Christian athlete *loses it* in a game or practice. A bad call from an official, a cheap shot from a player, or even a poor play on our part can cause us to allow our flesh to guide our actions. What comes out? The hidden pride and anger that compels us to complain, argue, swear, or give a cheap shot in retaliation. Is this the calling of a Christian athlete?

■　■　■

Justin, a college all-star basketball player and strong Christian, was in the conference championship game his senior year. He had been the go-to guy for the entire season and had proved over and over that he can produce under pressure. The game plan of the opposing team, of course, was to shut Justin down. In the first half, Justin had fifteen points, six rebounds, and five assists. He drew eight fouls, as he was either double-teamed or triple-teamed every time he got the ball. In the second half, he showed why he was an all-star by adding seventeen more points, including the game winner with two seconds left on the clock. The crowd was in awe at his performance on the court, but it was his character that was the focus of the comments in the stands. Like typical fans, many booed, jeered, and hassled the officials for perceived bad calls or no calls. However, through all of the yelling, the fans were firsthand eyewitnesses to Justin's reactions to the calls and hard fouls. After every call that went against him, Justin simply smiled. After every hard foul, a smile. After every cheap shot, there was a smile. Most of the fans were even unaware of the hidden pokes, the pinching of the flesh, and the sneaky hits below the belt that Justin had endured. All they saw was a young man playing his heart out with a smile on his face for the love of the game and to the honor of God. Can this be a true story? Are there truly athletes out there that have a godly character that will supersede any situation?

■　■　■

I believe that one of the reasons God placed us Christians in athletics is so we could show His character in competition. Although we may be physically beaten and bruised, it should be our goal to come out of the battle spiritually victorious with our testimony intact. This kind of character does not happen overnight. It takes discipline and intense preparation to stand firm under pressure. The Apostle Paul says it well.

✝ *It takes discipline and intense preparation to stand firm under pressure.*

Everyone who competes in the games goes into strict training. They do it to get a crown that will not last; but we do it to get a crown that will last forever. Therefore I do not run like a man running aimlessly; I do not fight like a man beating the air. No I beat my body and make it my slave so that after I have preached to others, I myself will not be disqualified for the prize.

I Corinthians 9:25–27 (NIV)

Dissecting this passage we see that there are two games addressed: the game of sport and the game of life. Paul highlights the similarity in preparation ("Everyone who competes in the games goes into *strict training*"), as well as the difference in the objective ("They do it to get a crown that will not last; but we do it to get a crown that will last forever."). It is important for us to see that as Christian athletes we must focus on character training even more than physical training. Although the physical training may help to win trophies (perishable), it is the character training that will help us to have godly actions in any circumstance so that we can ultimately win others to Christ (imperishable).

Evaluate Your Game

- What circumstances arise in my sport where I struggle to maintain godly character?

- What circumstances arise in my life where I struggle to maintain godly character?

- What practical things can I do to keep my focus on serving God?

Time-Out

Lord, forgive me for the times that I have allowed my circumstances to get in the way of my purpose, mission, and focus. Help me to maintain godly character and keep my eyes directly on You...no matter what obstacles I face.

PART FOUR

Dealing with Failure

I've failed over and over and over again in my life and that is why I succeed.

—Michael Jordan

Failure happens all the time. It happens every day in practice. What makes you better is how you react to it.

—Mia Hamm

THE AGONY OF DEFEAT

I was a high school varsity boy's soccer coach from 2003 to 2007. My teams in those years amassed seventy-two wins, twenty-three losses, and nine ties. Four times we made it to the state final-four, winning the state championship once. Of the twenty-three losses, there is one that stands out as the most painful. It was in the 2004 high school tournament. We were playing in the second round against the number one team in the district, the Pioneers. Although they were ranked ahead of us, most soccer enthusiasts had us as the heavy favorite.

The initial whistle blew, and my team went to work. We started off strong and picked them apart offensively. We penetrated into their defensive third of the field repeatedly and got off several solid shots, but their keeper was equal to the task, and he squelched all of our opportunities. Then the Pioneers got a little penetration into our defensive third and a miscue on our part allowed an opening on which they capitalized. We were down one to zero. There was still plenty of time, and we were dominating, so there was no need to panic. We kicked off and went back to work. We started pelting their goal with shots, but time was ticking away, and we could not get anything past their goalkeeper. The Pioneers got the ball on our half of the field once again and earned a free kick from about thirty-five yards out. They sent the ball into our goal box, and my keeper grabbed it out of the air, but as he came down, he lost control, and a Pioneer player was in the right place at the right time. He said, "Thank you very much." We were down two to zero.

Halftime—what do you tell a team that is totally dominating but down by two goals? I stayed positive and encouraged them to keep plugging away.

The second half began, and we came out shooting. Shot…save…shot, miss…shot…post…shot…*goooooooal!* We got one back with twenty-eight minutes left. I thought to myself, *That was all we needed.* The Pioneers kicked off, and we immediately took the ball away from them and went back to work, hammering their goal. Then a collision in their box left their incredible goalkeeper lame (later we found out he had a few broken ribs). He stayed in the game, but he was visibly shaken and struggling to move around. At that point, I knew we had the game won. With about ten minutes left, we scored again to tie it up two to two. Regulation time ends, and my team was fully confident that we would come out victorious. We played fifteen minutes of overtime and practically camped in front of their goal with no result. The second overtime began, and I anxiously waited to see who would score our winning goal. Shot…miss…shot…miss… shot…save. Time was running out on us, and it began to look like we were headed to a shoot-out. The Pioneers had one last run into our goal box with a minute left and earned a corner kick. Their kick sent the ball into our goal mouth, and we were scrambling to get it out. One of my defenders got his foot to the ball, and collectively our hearts sunk when our defender's kick did not clear the ball out of danger. In fact, he kicked the ball into our own goal. I was in shock. The players dropped in disbelief. We out shot that team thirty-four to eight and lost two to three. Our season was over.

We shook hands and congratulated the winning team. We then gathered around the center circle in the middle of the field for prayer, which was our tradition after every tournament game, win or lose. The two statements I made to my team were, "This stinks," and "I am hurting with you." I wanted my players to know that it was okay to hurt after a loss because the pain was real. We bowed our heads and cried out to God. That cry and all of the tears that were shed were directed to our Heavenly Father. That circle of prayer marked the end of our season, and yet it was an Abel's offering to the Lord of comfort.

> You're blessed when you feel you've lost what is most dear to you. Only then can you be embraced by the One most dear to you.
>
> Matthew 5:4 (The Message)

Too often after a heartbreaking loss I have heard it said, "It is just a game." I understand when looking at the big picture of life, yes, that is true. But that could be said for any type of loss whether it is a game, pet, boyfriend, or girlfriend. However, when you have invested blood, sweat, and tears and you are emotionally attached, then it is more than just a game.

God loves us, and He cares about every aspect of our

lives. I believe that He allows us to suffer loss so that we can look to Him for solace. Because not only is God with us in times of loss, but He *wants* to be with us in those times.

> Give all your worries and cares to God, for He cares about you.
>
> 1 Peter 5:7 (NLT)

Our Heavenly Coach understands our pain when we lose a game, and He desires to share that sorrow with us. He is our Rock, our Comforter, our Friend. May we seek to lean on Him when we experience the agony of defeat.

Evaluate Your Game

• Who do you go to for comfort when you fail or suffer defeat?

Time-Out

Lord, thank You for being my Comforter during the losses in my life. Use my sorrow to build strong character in me. Use my suffering to help strengthen and encourage others.

F.O.C.U.S.

Failure comes in many different forms at all levels of athletics. There are tiny failures that may cost you a point. There are larger failures that may cost you a game or an entire season. One thing is certain: everyone experiences failure.

I coached a U10 and a U11 boy's club soccer team for several years. It was interesting to see the reactions of those kids after a loss. Some of them cried, feeling that they were the ones responsible. Others pointed fingers and blamed the players who were on defense or the players who were on offense. Some laughed and were excited because the game was over, and they were going bowling afterwards. These ten- and eleven-year-old kids were learning to deal with the emotion involved with failure.

Emotion aside, failure is an essential ingredient for maturity. We have to understand that learning comes from failure, and if we can stay focused, we can turn failure into success. I call it the F.O.C.U.S. Principle: Fail, Own, Correct, Use, and Succeed. When you Fail, Own up and take responsibility for it, Correct your mistakes, then Use what you have learned to Succeed in the future. We will discuss the first two parts of this principle in this chapter and the final three in the next chapter.

Failure

Have you ever lost a game to someone who has never played the game before? I have, and it can be frustrating. Not necessarily because I had lost to a less experienced player, but sometimes I get irritated because the winning player is not as excited as he or she should be.

I have come to realize that the reason for the lack of excitement on the part of the novice victor is because the victory came with no reference to a struggle to win. Since they had never played the game before, they lack the experience of losing it, and thus miss a sense of accomplishment.

My boys enjoy playing video games. When they have game controllers in their hands, they bounce, twist, and lean as if they can influence the characters in the game with their body movement. I often hear them in their playroom screaming and crying out with intense emotion as they fail time and time again to beat a certain level of the game. But once in a while, my boys will race upstairs from the playroom to inform me that they had succeeded and passed a level that they had never beaten before. They get so excited. Why? I contend that it is all due to failure. Even though they were losing most of the time, they were totally engaged into the video game because they enjoyed the challenge. When they finally broke through and won after repeated failure, they had defeated two giants: the foe of the game and the foe of failure itself.

✝ *...the joy of success is dependent on failure.*

Failure is inevitable, but I believe the joy of success is dependent on failure. Instead of dwelling on the disappointment of failure, embrace the experience as an opportunity to grow. Consider the words of James.

> Dear brothers and sisters, when troubles come your way, consider it an opportunity for great joy. For you know that when your faith is tested, your endurance has a chance to grow. So let it grow, for when your endurance is fully developed, you will be perfect and complete, needing nothing.
>
> James 1:2–4 (NLT)

Our view about failure must be a positive one. Be assured that you will fail many times, but it is not the failure that matters to God as much as how you handle the failure.

Owning Up

Three of the hardest words to say are, "I was wrong." I am not sure why it is so tough to admit when we are wrong or that we make mistakes. I think it is because we, especially us athletes, see everything as a competition; and when we admit we are wrong, we think we have lost. Our minds need to be reprogrammed. Everything *is* a competition, but our battle is not against flesh and blood.

† *Everything is a competition, but our battle is not against flesh and blood.*

Put on the full armor of God so that you can take your stand against the devil's schemes. For our struggle is not against flesh and blood, but against the rulers, against the authorities, against the powers of this dark world and against the spiritual forces of evil in the heavenly realms.

Ephesians 6:11–12 (NIV)

According to these verses our opponent is the devil himself, and we are to take our stand against his schemes. When we refuse to admit our mistakes, we start to lose our focus, and we fall right into our opponent's game plan. Let's look at the story of Cain and Abel again.

"Why are you so angry?" the Lord asked Cain. "Why do you look so dejected? You will be accepted if you do what is right. But if you refuse to do what is right, then watch out! Sin is crouching at the door, eager to control you. But you must subdue it and be its master."

Gen. 4:6, 7 (NLT)

God gives us some wise counsel here. If we do not own up to our mistakes and admit when we are wrong, we invite sin to take over—we turn the ball over to the other team. Cain did not heed the Lord's advice. Consider what happened next.

One day Cain suggested to his brother, "Let's go out into the fields." And while they were in the field, Cain attacked his brother, Abel, and killed him.

Gen 4:8(NLT)

What caused Cain to kill his brother? Cain didn't do what was right in the sight of the Lord. Abel did, and it made Cain angry. His anger consumed him, and despite the Lord's warning, he did not subdue it, nor did he master it. Owning up to our failures is not easy, but it is absolutely necessary.

Satan understands our desire to succeed. Part of his game plan is for us to define success in a way that reflects our human desires and not the Lord's desires. True success requires us to die to self. We have to be willing to let go of our human desires in order to attain heavenly goals. Cain's human desire was to keep the best crop for himself.

I have often wondered what would have happened if Cain said, "You are right, Lord; forgive me. Here is the best of my crop." It seems so simple, an easy problem to correct. But for Cain to say those words meant he was saying: Abel one–Cain zero. He had to admit failure, and his ego would not let him do that.

Why is it so tough to admit failure? I believe it is because our flesh seeks competition rather than collaboration. It is especially difficult for athletes who are trained to compete. From games on the playing field to grades in the classroom, to passing cars in traffic, we often see everyday situations as competitions. When a competitive person views a mistake as failure and sees failure as losing, then he or she is reluctant to admit that they made a mistake. They may get angry and put themselves in a position where, as the Lord put it, "sin will be crouching at the door."

We must heed the Lord's advice to Cain and master the anger and frustration that surfaces because of our failures. The first step in doing this is to own up to our mistakes.

Evaluate Your Game

- What are some areas in my sport where I am prone to fail?
- When is it hard for me to admit failure?
- Is it easier for me to blame others for my failure or own up to it?

Time-Out

Lord, help me to stay focused. Give me a humble heart, and grant me wisdom to deal with my failures in a manner worthy of You.

LEARNING FROM FAILURE

Owning up to our mistakes is the hardest step in the process of overcoming failure; however, the correction step is the most important and requires the most effort on our part. For example, if you play tennis and you have a problem keeping your first serve in play, then what would you do to correct that problem? The fierce competitor goes out on to the court and spends hours working on his or her serve until they get it right and their first-service percentage improves. Correction is not easy. It takes time and energy, but the benefits are extremely rewarding.

Some mistakes are easier to correct than others. I think the hardest type of correction is when we have to swallow our pride and fix a mistake we have made against another person. These kinds of mistakes occur often in sports. We sometimes refer to it as emotion in the heat of the moment. Regardless of the reason, once we have failed to represent Christ and we emotionally, psychologically, or even physically injure another person because of a lack of our own self-control, we must obey the Spirit and correct that mistake. As I said before, it is not easy. But we are commanded by our Lord to do all we can to make amends and fix our faults.

Do all that you can to live in peace with everyone.

Romans 12:18 (NLT)

Almost every year of my coaching career, at least two of my key players have developed a strained relationship during the season. Frustration sets in, and someone says or does something to start the conflict that will undoubtedly hurt the entire team if not dealt with. Dealing with it involves walking through the F.O.C.U.S steps. I have found that if my players can admit failure, own up, and accept part of the responsibility for the conflict, then they can usually come up with their own ways to correct the mistakes that were made and begin to repair the relationship.

The fact that correction takes place in our lives is evidence of our spiritual growth. It is at this step that we do all of our brainstorming to come up with ways to make something better. And when we make something better, we make ourselves better. It is during the disciplined process of correcting a mistake when we actually acquire knowledge and wisdom. As the wisest man who ever lived once said,

> To learn, you must love discipline; it is stupid to hate correction.
>
> Proverbs 12:1 (NLT)

Using Failure

One of my favorite awards to give as a coach was the most improved player award. This would be awarded to the athlete who had greatly improved his or her skills by using their corrections of early failures to grow their game. When any coach sees a player working hard to improve and sees that hard work pay off by raising the player's level of play, it always gives the coach immense joy. This is similar to our Christian walk. I believe our Heavenly Coach feels joy when He sees us grow and improve our spiritual lives. When we correct mistakes we have made and make a conscience effort to use what we learn to make lifestyle changes that are pleasing to the Lord, He rejoices.

We are reminded of His joy throughout the New Testament. Jesus told this story:

> If a man has a hundred sheep and one of them gets lost, what will he do? Won't he leave the ninety-nine others in the wilderness and go to search for the one that is lost until he finds it? And when he has found it, he will joyfully carry it home on his shoulders. When he arrives, he will call together his friends and neighbors, saying, "Rejoice with me because I have found my lost sheep." In the same way, there is more joy in heaven over one lost sinner who repents and returns to God than over ninety-nine others who are righteous and haven't strayed away!
>
> Luke 15:4–7 (NLT)

Our Heavenly Coach desires to give us the most improved award, and He will do all that he can to help us. Paul says:

> And I am certain that God, who began the good work within you, will continue his work until it

is finally finished on the day when Christ Jesus returns.

> Philippians 1:6 (NLT)

He will do His part. It is our job to use what we have learned from the experiences that God takes us through to increase our knowledge of Him and raise our level of play in all of the areas of our lives.

Success

Most people see winning games or scoring points as the measure of athletic success. As Christians, however, we must understand how God measures success.

> But the LORD said to Samuel, "Do not look at his appearance or his stature, because I have rejected him. Man does not see what the LORD sees, for man sees what is visible, but the LORD sees the heart."
>
> 1 Samuel 16:7 (HCSB)

When God chose David to be the future king of His people, He saw that David was mentally and physically capable, but most importantly, He saw that David also had the invisible qualities of the heart that are necessary for a successful ruler.

Success is not based on achievements, honors, or awards. God says that He looks at the condition of our hearts. Most coaches, officials, and fans would like to say the same. We are always preaching character, integrity, and honesty in sports. We lump these invisible qualities under the term *sportsmanship*. We also desire to see our athletes to show *heart* as part of their character. By this I mean we want them to demonstrate determination, drive, and mental toughness along with good sportsmanship. I have found that when an athlete shows strong Christian character coupled with a big heart, he or she is often crowned with earthly success as well as heavenly success.

We must focus our attention on developing the invisible qualities of the heart and strive for heavenly rewards. Therein lay the secret to success in the eyes of God. Jesus tells us that we do not need to worry about anything on this earth. I believe that includes winning and losing. In His words:

> Seek the Kingdom of God above all else, and live righteously, and He will give you everything you need.
>
> Matthew 6:33(NLT)

True success is found in seeking the Kingdom of God. With that as our goal, we must apply the F.O.C.U.S. Principle to all the areas of our lives and turn our failures into heavenly success. When we Fail, let's Own up and take responsibility to Correct our mistakes and Use what we have learned to Succeed. Live righteously, and He will give us everything we need.

Evaluate Your Game

- Do I use my failures as a tool to grow or as an excuse to give up?
- Does my view of success reflect God's view of success?

Time-Out

Lord, as I work to correct and use my mistakes, I call on Your promise that You will be faithful to complete the good work that you started in me. Thank You for Your desire to see me be successful in You.

PART FIVE

Power Up

Jesus replied, "Anyone who drinks this water will soon become thirsty again. But those who drink the water I give will never be thirsty again. It becomes a fresh, bubbling spring within them, giving them eternal life."

John 4:13–14 (NIV)

The time when there is no one there to feel sorry for you or to cheer for you is when a player is made.

—Tim Duncan

LIKE CHRIST

Some of you are old enough to remember Michael Jordan in the Gatorade commercials where everyone wanted to be *like Mike*. At that time, Michael Jordan was the best there was in the NBA. He had it all—talent, money, respect, and championship rings.

As Christians, it is important that we set our focus on the goal of being *like Christ*. After all, our main purpose on this earth is to be an extension of Christ. This should be easy, for it is who we are. When we accepted Jesus Christ as Savior, we committed ourselves to be His ambassadors. We bear the name of Christ wherever we are. We are Christian coaches, Christian fans, and Christian athletes. Therefore, it is our obligation to be models of Christ and seek His will in our sports.

† *...what good is it to play hard and win trophies when you act like a jerk?*

I like the slogan I have seen on many athletic T-shirts. It says, "Play Hard or Go Home." That always gets my competitive juices flowing. But, there is more to it for the Christian competitor. For us, the phrase should read, "Play Hard, Be Christ, or Go Home." Think about it, what good is it to play hard and win trophies when you act like a jerk? We are supposed to exhibit Christ, so unless we think Christ is a jerk, we defeat our true purpose for competing. When our teammates, fans, officials, and opponents observe us in athletics, they should see Christ through us. They should see us bearing His fruit.

> I am the True Vine and my Father is the gardener. He cuts off every branch in me that bears no fruit, while every branch that does bear fruit, He prunes so that it will be even more fruitful.
>
> John 15:1–2 (NIV)

> This is to my Father's glory, that you bear much fruit, showing yourselves to be my disciples.
>
> John 15:8 (NIV)

As believers we are branches of Jesus Christ, the True Vine. The purpose of the branch is to bear fruit, and if it is not bearing fruit, then the branch is worthless. I found it interesting looking at the passages in John 15 that Jesus, the Vine, does not bear fruit. Fruit is produced only on the branches of the vine. We are the manifestations of God's character. We are the branches, and it is our job to bear (showcase) the fruit of Christ and demonstrate His character in our sports.

When we make it a goal to exhibit Christ and bear His fruit and we allow ourselves to be led by the Holy Spirit, then we will live out the character that God intended for us to display. That is when we are at our best.

Bearing fruit does not happen overnight. It takes discipline and effort on our part as we allow the Father to work in our lives. He prunes us so that we will be more fruitful.

> But the fruit of the Spirit is love, joy, peace, patience, kindness, goodness, faithfulness, gentleness, and self-control. Against such thing there is no law.
>
> Galatians 5:22–23 NIV

> So I say live by the Spirit, and you will not gratify the desires of the sinful nature.
>
> Galatians 5:16 NIV

Everything we need to live a life worthy of Christ can be found in the Holy Spirit. By tapping into this everlasting resource, we manifest the attributes of God, bearing the fruits of the True Vine.

In the next few chapters we will dissect the fruits of the Spirit individually and look at some small things that we can do to develop these fruits in the athletic arena.

Evaluate Your Game

- How can I be more *like Christ* in my sport?
- What steps do I need to take to be continually led by the Spirit?

Time-Out

Lord, help me to demonstrate Your character to all those around me. May they see You in me as I seek to be like Christ.

POWER-AIDE

There are an abundance of sports drinks that are designed to give us some sort of a boost: Gatorade, POWERade$_{TM}$, Propel, Amp, Red Bull, or Full Throttle. They all boast of providing the benefits of hydration, energy, endurance, or nutrient replacement. We can look at the Holy Spirit as being our spiritual Power-Aide. If we look closely at the benefits we would gain from consuming Him, we would find love, joy, peace, patience, kindness, goodness, faithfulness, gentleness, and self-control. These qualities are not only beneficial for this life, but will last throughout eternity.

Goodness & Faithfulness

> His master replied, "Well done, good and faithful servant! You have been faithful with a few things; I will put you in charge of many things. Come and share your master's happiness!"
>
> Matthew 25:21 (NIV)

We talked about the parable of the talents in Chapters 3 and 4. Let's look at it again. Notice from the praise of the Master in Matthew 25:21 that the servant in this part of the parable was noted to have two fruits of the Spirit, goodness and faithfulness. I looked up the terms "good" and "faithful" in the dictionary to get an idea of the full scope of these words of praise. Here are highlights of what I found:

Good:

Effective, beneficial, clever, genuine, vigorous, honorable, worthy, respectable, desirable, dependable, reliable, virtuous, and honest.

Faithful:

Constant, loyal, steadfast, dutiful, responsible, conscientious, trustworthy, unwavering, determined, and undeviating allegiance

Wow, there is a lot packed into those two words. Imagine the energy boost you would supply to your teammates, coaches, opponents, and fans by being a good and faithful servant on the court or field, on the bench or in the locker room.

Make it a personal goal to exhibit the expanded description of these words. Daily, work to develop a heart that models the five and two-talent servants, so at the end of each day, practice, or game, you will be worthy to be called good and faithful.

Joy

Our commitment to be good and faithful allows us to experience joy in Christ. Contrary to popular thought, joy is not about having a good feeling or a sense of happiness, although they can be a part of it. Joy is the peace of knowing that no matter what the situation, the Lord is in complete control, and He always has our best interest in mind. That is why James can say:

> Consider it pure joy, my brothers, when you face trials of many kinds. Because you know that the testing of your faith develops perseverance.
>
> James 1:2–3 (NIV)

The understanding of God's sovereignty is what can put a smile on your face and keep you going when things are tough. The next time you are in the middle of a taxing game or grueling practice, take a mental pause to praise the Lord, and take a sip from your spiritual Power-Aide. Thank Him for the tough time because you know that it is helping you to develop perseverance. Experience the joy and smile. Then finish strong!

Evaluate Your Game

- What can I do to be a good and faithful servant in the sports arena?
- How can I show the joy of the Lord in my sport?

Time-Out

Lord, I desire the true joy that can only come from you. Help me to be a good and faithful servant and bless me with Your peace.

FRUIT$_4$U

I was dying of thirst after an *over thirty* league soccer game. I ran out of water on a humid ninety-degree day, so on the way home, I stopped at a convenient store, looking for something to replenish the liters of water that I had lost in the game. I anticipated just getting a bottle of water, but the store had a special on Fruit$_2$O$_{TM}$, so I tried it. Not bad. It boasts of being a refreshing, no-calorie, natural spring water with a splash of fruit taste. What a neat analogy for us as Christian athletes. We should be refreshing, natural, and flavored with the fruits of the Spirit so that through us, others can sample the wellspring of goodness from our God.

> Taste and see that the Lord is good. Oh, the joys of those who take refuge in him!
> Psalm 34:8 (NLT)

Let's look at some of the fruits of the Spirit that focus on our relationships with others.

Patience & Peace

† *It is through your acts of patience that God blesses you with peace.*

Patience and peace go hand in hand. It is through your acts of patience that God blesses you with peace.

Do not be anxious about anything, but in everything, by prayer and petition, with thanksgiving, present your requests to God. And the peace of God, which transcends all understanding, will guard your hearts and minds in Christ Jesus.

Philippians 4:6–7 (NIV)

Peace is a two-part fruit. There is inner peace, a refuge based on our relationship with God, knowing that we have a God that is bigger than any problem, situation, or game. There is also a more visible community peace that is found in the relationship we have with others. This is where we demonstrate the ability to turn away wrath and elicit calmness during tense situations. It is the acceptance of God's inner peace in your life and the repeated acts of patience that allows you to grow the fruit of community peace.

■　■　■

I can remember my first time golfing on a real golf course. I was in high school with a few of my buddies who were all fairly avid golfers. I was unbeatable on the Putt-Putt course, so I figured how hard could it be? Well, if you want to work on your inner peace, take up golf. When I was up to tee off on the first hole, it seemed like everybody and their brother gathered around to watch. I was so nervous. I did a warm up routine that I picked up watching the golfers in the group that teed off before us—I took a few practice swings, set my feet, and looked at my target and then at the ball. I was ready. I had a perfect backswing and a powerful frontswing (I know that is not a golfing term, but I don't know what to call it). I missed the ball. Of course I played it off as being just another practice swing. I tried again, now more nervous than ever. The second time I made contact, and the ball sailed 350…centimeters. I felt a collective sigh from all of the golfers behind me waiting to get on to the course. I prayed, *Lord give all those golfers a heavy dose of patience today.* I spent more time replacing divots and searching through the woods for my ball than I did actually golfing, but I made it through.

■   ■   ■

There is such a void of patience and peace in sports today. We need to consume gallons of spiritual water containing these fruits. We live in such a "grass is greener," "get it now," "it's all about me" society that these fruits are slowly drying up.

To produce patience and peace in our sports, we must heed the words of the Apostle Paul in Philippians, chapter 4. He said that we must go to God in prayer, and petition Him with thanksgiving.

You may be in a situation where you are forced to exercise patience. You may be waiting to get playing time or to break into the starting lineup. You may be in a performance slump and you are chomping at the bit ready to get out of it. You may find yourself in conflict with a teammate, opponent, or coach. Hang in there, go to God in prayer, take a sip of His spiritual Fruit U, and He will give you a peace that transcends all understanding and refreshes you so that you can be a refreshment to others.

Kindness & Gentleness

The best way to look at the fruits of kindness and gentleness is to highlight the destructiveness of the opposites of those terms. The opposite of kindness is cruelty. The opposite of gentleness is abusiveness. In the heated moments of the games we play, we are constantly faced with the decision to be kind when we want to be cruel and to be gentle when we want to be abusive.

It is our nature to want justice and seek revenge when we feel like we have been wronged. But we are *Christian* athletes, Christ's ambassadors on this earth. Thus, we must look at the wrongs we suffer with heavenly vision.

> To you who are ready for the truth, I say this: Love your enemies. Let them bring out the best in you, not the worst. When someone gives you a hard time, respond with the energies of prayer for that person. If someone slaps you in the face, stand there and take it. If someone grabs your shirt, gift-wrap your best coat and make a present of it. If someone takes unfair advantage of you, use the occasion to practice the servant life. No more tit-for-tat stuff. Live generously.
>
> Luke 6:27–30 (Message)

If someone hits you, don't hit back? This is so counter to our nature, especially for athletes who are focused on winning and trained to be aggressive and competitive. As much as we might want to, we cannot argue with the Word. Loving our enemies is not only what Jesus commanded in Luke 6:27, but also what He demonstrated when He was verbally abused, spit upon, and beat to a pulp before He was finally crucified for our sins. Not once did Jesus retaliate. Wow. That takes strength.

We have to trust that God will take care of the wrongs we suffer—in His time, using His methods. He promises that He will handle the justice.

> Don't hit back; discover beauty in everyone. If you've got it in you, get along with everybody. Don't insist on getting even; that's not for you to do. "I'll do the judging," says God. "I'll take care of it."
>
> Romans 12:17–19 (Message)

To ripen the sweet fruits of kindness and gentleness as opposed to the bitterness of cruelty and abusiveness requires an adjustment in our minds as to how we view others. We must see our teammates, opponents, officials, and fans as Christ sees them. They are people who matter to Him. They are uniquely created by Him and for Him. He loves them; therefore, we must love them too. They are thirsty for Christ, so let us provide them with the refreshing water of Christ's love splashed with the fruits of kindness and gentleness.

Evaluate Your Game

- What are some practical ways for me to demonstrate patience and to be at peace with all men?
- What can I do to demonstrate kindness and gentleness in my sport?

Time-Out

Lord, thank You for showing me how to act. You are so patient with me, and Your kindness is everlasting. Help me to exhibit these fruits in my life.

DARE TO LOVE

Am I now trying to get people to think well of me? Or do I want God to think well of me? Am I trying to please people? If I were, I would not be serving Christ.

Galatians 1:10 (NIRV)

Self-control

As we allow the Spirit to work in our lives and allow His fruits to mature in us, we automatically gain more control over our sinful nature by handing over the controls to God. Self-control is a manifestation of the fruit of faithfulness. If we pledge our allegiance to our Savior, we die to self, and thus we have the ability to control self. This type of control requires us to make daily decisions to be God pleasing rather than people pleasing or self pleasing.

Coaching high school boys in the past gave me a front seat to watch the *Sin Nature vs. Spirit* control battle. I did my best to try and prepare my players for this internal war. Before games, I had my players do some visualization exercises. I had them sit quietly, close their eyes, and picture in their minds different situations that may occur during the course of the game. I would ask them to focus specifically on an area of weakness (i.e., anger management) and visualize the occurrence of a situation that causes them to stumble in that area (i.e., a poor call from an official). Next, I would have them visualize themselves handling the situation as Christ would. It is crucial to anticipate temptation and plan for it. We conquer half the control battle by not being caught off guard.

✝ *It is crucial to anticipate temptation and plan for it*

Dear friends, I warn you as "temporary residents and foreigners" to keep away from worldly desires that wage war against your very souls. Be careful to live properly among your unbelieving neighbors. Then even if they accuse you of doing wrong, they will see your honorable behavior, and they will give honor to God when he judges the world.

1 Peter 2:11–12 (NLT)

Decide now to be firmly connected to the True Vine. Let His energy flow through you so that you will produce the sweet fruits of the Spirit. Allow yourself to be controlled by the Spirit, and let the world around you sample His fruits through you that they may taste and see that the Lord is good.

Love

I remember when food companies first started manufacturing sophisticated fruit drinks by combining juices that I would never have thought to combine. Sipping on drinks like Kiwi-Strawberry, Mango-Orange, or Orange-Strawberry-Banana made me feel like I was special–drinking high-class drinks. The fruit of Love could be considered like one of these blended drinks, for it encompasses all of the fruits of the Spirit. It is the sharing of this fruit that reveals to others that we are Christians.

> A new command I give you: Love one another. As I have loved you, so you must love one another. By this all men will know that you are my disciples, if you love one another.
>
> John 13:34–35 (NIV)

It is our love that will expose Christ to our teammates, officials, coaches, fans, and opponents. It is our duty as God's children to love each person whom we come in contact with as Christ does.

> Dear friends, let us love one another, for love comes from God. Everyone who loves has been born of God and knows God. Whoever does not love does not know God, because God is love.
>
> 1 John 4:7–8 (NIV)

Paul explains it so well in 1 Corinthians 13. It is easy to see in this passage of scripture the application of love for the Christian in the area of sports. Read it slowly.

> Love is patient, love is kind. It does not envy, it does not boast, it is not proud. It is not rude, it is not self-seeking, it is not easily angered, it keeps no record of wrongs. Love does not delight in evil but rejoices with the truth. It always protects, always trusts, always hopes, always perseveres.
>
> 1 Corinthians 13:4–7 (NIV)

To love is the ultimate spiritual goal. Let us daily strive to be *like Christ* by choosing to love. Let us show ourselves to be worthy of His high calling.

Evaluate Your Game

- What fruits of the Spirit do I exhibit most in my sport?
- What fruits of the Spirit do I need to work on?
- In my sport, who needs to be touched by my love?

Time-Out

Lord, thank you for loving me so much. Help me to show that same love to others.

PART SIX

Sweet Victory

Take your victories, whatever they may be, cherish them, use them, but don't settle for them.

—Mia Hamm

When you have tasted disappointment, it makes success that much sweeter.

—Tony Dungy

THE THRILL OF VICTORY

I remember it well. It was Saturday, May 6, 1989, my sophomore year in college. I was one of eight anchor-legs from around the country who was set to help his 4 x 400 meter relay team win the national title. My heart raced, and I could feel the surge of adrenaline pumping through each artery of my body, preparing every system to work at maximum capacity. I visualized the baton exchange, focusing on my drive and the pass. I was almost ready—almost, because I always had a relaxing yawn before a race, and it had not happened yet. I went through my routine of jumping up and down, shaking out my legs and arms, and taking a few deep breaths as I waited to see what position my teammate would be in as he entered the homestretch. It was second. I thought, *I have one to beat.* I was in a similar situation in high school during state qualifications. I came within inches, but I failed to beat the one person that I needed to beat to propel my team to the state meet. I was determined not to let that happen again. The official placed us in our lanes for the baton exchange. I raised my hand to help my teammate locate me, and I said a quick prayer: "Lord, give me strength. This is for you." I yawned. As my teammate entered the exchange zone, I took four hard driving strides, turned, and reached back with my left hand to grab the stick. The pass was perfect. I turned, switched the baton to my right hand, and focused on my goal. I remember being totally relaxed, breathing steadily, and drafting my opponent. When we hit the middle of the backstretch, I said to myself, "*Now!*" and I started to kick. A deep inhale and a powerful exhale turned on the mental switch that shifted the gears of my body and told my muscle fibers to "pick it up." My strides instantly increased in length and repetition as I surged past my opponent just before we hit the final curve. I visually told the field, "If he is going to meet my challenge, then he is going to have to do it in the outside lane." As I entered the final straight away, I could feel my opponents falling behind. I began to prepare myself for the next obstacle, *the monkey.* This mental nuisance usually climbs on my back with seventy-five meters to go, and he makes my legs feel like they each weigh one-hundred pounds. The only way to fight him off is by maintaining good form. "Relax, stay loose, breathe, pump your arms." I was repeating all the words that were branded in my head since the first time the monkey and I were introduced. I hit the seventy-five-meter mark. My brain did a quick body scan and reported no sign of the monkey. At sixty-five meters, still no monkey. "Yes!" It doesn't happen often, but occasionally, the monkey is not up to the challenge and decides to lie off. I shifted into overdrive, and at that moment, I felt like Eric Liddell in the movie, *Chariots of Fire*[5] when he said, "I believe God made me for a purpose, but he also made me fast. And when I run, I feel His pleasure." In the film, Eric is running in the midst of a roaring crowd, but the entire din is silent, and all of the surrounding scenery is viewed in slow motion as that quote is being delivered. That is how I felt. Everything seemed to slow down as I powered to the finish line. I heard nothing but the sound of my spikes piercing the rubber on the track, and I crossed the finish line a national champion.

As I recall that race, I cannot help but think of all the good times and of all the bad times that led up to that moment. As I reflect on all of the lessons that I have learned through sports, I contemplate on the times I had to deal with failure, and I assess all of the positive and negative intangibles that had a part in shaping my career as a Christian athlete. I cannot help but to praise God for granting me the talents and opportunities to compete throughout the years.

Not all athletes get to experience the thrill of winning a championship in an earthly competition, but the thrill of victory is experienced by all Christians. The *monkey of sin* that wants to jump on our backs and overpower us is no match for our Savior who conquered death by shedding his blood on a cross.

> The sting of death is sin, and the power of sin is the law. But thanks be to God! He gives us the victory through our Lord Jesus Christ. Therefore, my dear brothers, stand firm. Let nothing move you. Always give yourselves fully to the work of the Lord, because you know that your labor in the Lord is not in vain.
>
> I Corinthians 15:56–58. (NIV)

Press on. Stay focused on your spiritual goals and be

faithful. You have been created with incredible talents. Use those gifts and abilities in your sport and in your life to bring glory to your Creator. Continue to learn and grow from the experiences that God blesses you with, knowing that you will be rewarded as your knowledge turns into wisdom and your wisdom turns into victories over sin. And may we anticipate the future thrill of our ultimate victory when our Lord and Savior returns.

Let me close this book by praying a prayer for you. This is one of Paul's prayers that he prayed for the Thessalonians:

> With this in mind, we constantly pray for you, that our God may count you worthy of His calling, and that by His power He may fulfill every good purpose of yours and every act prompted by your faith. We pray this so that the name of our Lord Jesus may be glorified in you, and you in Him, according to the grace of our God and the Lord Jesus Christ.
>
> 2Thessalonians 1:12(NIV)

Endnotes

Photographs provided by Anne Marie Weakley

1   Rudy–by Tristar Pictures, Fried/Woods Films Production on Columbia Tristar Video, 3400 riverside Dr. Burbank CA 91505, 1993.

2   Remo Williams: The Adventure begins–by Metro Goldwyn Mayer Studios, 10250 Constellation Blvd., Los Angeles CA 90067, 1985.

3   Purpose Driven Life: What on earth am I here for?– by Rick Warren, published by Zondervan, Grand Rapids MI, Copyright © 2000, p.89

4   All Things Are Possible–by Kurt Warner with Michael Silver, published by HarperCollins Publishers, Inc., New York New York, Copyright © 2000, pp.17,18

5   Chariots of Fire–by Ladd Company and Warner Brothers, Warner Home Video, Inc., 4000 Warner Blvd. Burbank, CA 91522, 1986